The Modern

"A" FRAME SKI TECHNIQUE

An expedient pocket or digital guide for Alpine and Telemark skiing for novice through expert skiers

Bill Hernon

Available in Soft Cover and Ebook Formats

Bill Hernon's
Modern "A" Frame Ski Technique
Copyright ©2019
All rights reserved.

Photos by Lyric Sylvan (lyricsylvan@gmail.com) and Lukaiel Reece-Sullivan (lukaielreecesullivan@gmail.com)
Skiers: Bill Hernon, Lyric Sylvan, and Meadow Sylvan

The Modern "A" Frame Ski Technique
May be Ordered From:
www.skiaframe.com/pocketguide

ISBN #978-1-7923-2596-0

DEDICATION

*This pocket guide is dedicated
to those who have skied before us
and to those who will ski after us.*

Bill's love of skiing inspired him to write this pocket guide to help skiers advance their ability as quickly and efficiently as possible. Using the **THE MODERN "A" FRAME SKI TECHNIQUE** will help anyone who wants to go skiing. It makes advanced and expert skiing possible for anyone who wants to make skiing a part of their life, for life! And the more proficient skiers become, the more they will enjoy their skiing experience and the more likely the art and sport of skiing will continue to thrive.

Wishing you the best on the mountain. Bill Hernon – bill@skiaframe.com

This pocket guide is written to help skiers advance their ability as quickly and efficiently as possible.

My love of skiing has prompted me to put this teaching method in print. The more skiers at the advanced to expert level, the more likely the art and sport of skiing will continue to thrive.

If you have never been on skis before, a few lessons from a professional ski instructor is highly recommended. It is important to have a basic understanding of the foundational elements of skiing.

The *wedge* or snowplow turn is the foundational concept on which skiing is built. It is that foundation on which we are going to build.

The difference between a *wedge* turn and an advanced *parallel* turn is not complicated. However, if the distance from beginner to advanced is about an inch, the distance from advanced to expert is a mile. *Bill Hernon's Modern "A" Frame Ski Technique* explains and expedites that process.

This pocket guide is a condensed and precise explanation of the *"A" Frame Ski Technique* and why it works. It is recommended that you should further explore ski equipment design, the human body, the snow and the mountain to truly grasp how they all work and interact.

As your abilities progress, it is important to be educated about the mountain, snow, avalanche conditions and safety. Professional instruction is available and is recommended.

The mountains are an amazing, beautiful and potentially dangerous place to play. Please show them the respect they deserve.

The term *"A" Frame* has been around for many years. My first experience with it was in the early 1980's. What follows is my refined version of that technique. It is my personal experience and my professional opinion, that use of this technique is the most effective way to excel at skiing.

From the foundation of the *"A" Frame Ski Technique*, the skier readily progresses into all forms of skiing such as *slalom*, *giant slalom*, *freestyle*, *powder* and *telemark* turns.

The *"A" Frame* body position is the basic athletic stance for athletes of all types modified for the skier to slide down a snowy hill on skis. I have condensed how and why the human body interacts with the equipment and the mountain into seven points to create the act of skiing.

Your Skis - The First Two "A's"

The sidecut of a ski creates an hourglass shape, or two inverted "A's". A ski is wider at the tip and tail then narrows in the center. When a ski is put on edge and pressured it turns by design. How one distributes their weight and pressures the ski controls how the ski will carve the turn. Forward pressure created by flexing into the front of the ski boot while angulating the outside or both knees into the turn starts the act of carving and turning the skis. (Angulation is the act of tilting your leg and or hips into the turn.) As one shifts weight or extends out of the turn the pressure moves from the front of the ski to the center and then to the tail completing the carve. All of this is done in the front seat, don't lean back.

The Wedge or Snowplow - The Third "A"

A perfect *wedge* stance is the foundation of skiing. It is the foundational position in which you ski. The differences between a *wedge* turn and a *parallel* turn are: 1) Independent leg action – to which ski you are applying your pressure and weight. In a *parallel* turn, most or all of your weight gets transferred to your outside or downhill ski. 2) Separation of the upper body from the lower body. This means your hands, shoulders, upper hips and eyes always face downhill, down the *fall line* and the lower body and skis turn across the hill. 3) *Flexion* and *extension*, the flexing and extention of the legs applies and releases preasure to the skis. When carving medium radius turns, think about peddling a bike.

It is these three key actions that take you from the *wedge* turn to the *parallel* turn. In many situations, it is okay if a small wedge or "A" occurs in your turn transition.

A great drill and stepping stone to help get to that parallel turn is the *stem christie* or step turn. This maneuver is less frequently taught in the USA. However, I think it is a crucial element in advanced to expert free skiing. In this maneuver, the downhill or outside ski's uphill edge holds the carve. You step the tail of the uphill, or inside ski, up and out, as you are unweighting and shifting weight by extending your downhill leg. If the upper body, hands, shoulders, upper hips and eyes are pointed downhill, the tips of your skis will naturally turn down the hill. You then flex into the front of your downhill boot and pressure your weight down and forward, angulating your knee into the hill, to carve the turn. This is not just a drill. This maneuver is used often in expert skiing terrain and conditions and is an excellent example of independent leg action.

The Feet to the Knees – The Fourth "A"

The leg from the foot to the knee is where knee angulation is created. The feet are slightly to fairly far apart depending on how low your hip is to the snow. The lower your hip is, the wider your skis will be apart. The outside/downhill knee tilts in towards the inside/uphill knee. This position tilts the outside/downhill ski onto its inside edge allowing the ski to carve a turn. This maneuver is critical to carving a turn. In many circumstances and conditions a skier has weight and pressure on both skis. In these situations you would tilt both knees into the hill. A *giant slalom* turn is a good example of this. Knowing how much pressure to apply to each ski will come with experience. If your skis are not carving this may solve your dilemma.

The Knees to the Hips – The Fifth "A"

This fifth "A" is a little hard to see, being it is inverted. However, the knees to the hips generally create an "A". The first five lower "A's" (lower body and skis) are what cross the *fall line* and rotate in the direction you are turning. The last two "A's", 6 and 7, always point down hill or down the *fall line*. Just above this fifth "A", at our waist, is the pivot point of the body. This is where we separate the upper body from the lower body when we turn the skis.

Keep your hips forward throughout the turn. This centers your weight forward on the ski and helps with forward pressure on your boots.

The Waist to the Shoulders – the Sixth "A"

Depending on your body build, this sixth "A" can be right side up or upside down. It doesn't matter, the separation of the upper body and lower body occurs at your waist. This "A" is to be pointed down the hill/ *fall line*. The shoulders should be kept perpendicular to the *fall line*. This is extremely important in advance and steep terrain. By aiming your upper body downhill you are working with gravity. This makes it easier to turn the skis. The separation between the upper and lower body also creates hip angulation. Hip angulation plus knee angulation is how you really lay it over to carve a turn.

If this "A" is upside down, meaning the body is wider at the shoulders than the hips, when you flex forward and down on your boots your weight tends to fall in front of your feet. If this "A" is right side up, meaning the body is wider at the hips than at the shoulders, when you flex forward and down on your boots the weight tends to fall to your feet.

This is the big difference between male and female skiers. The ski and boot manufacturing companies have taken this into account and you should shop for your personal build.

The Hands and the Poles – the Seventh "A"

The hands are very powerful gravity and centering points of the human body. The importance of their position within skiing technique cannot be overstated. It is crucial to have the hands at mid torso height, directed downhill and kept as calm as possible.

By simply dropping a hand to your side after the pole plant you have adversely altered your center of gravity. With the hand dropped, the shoulder has now dropped and you are no longer facing all of your upper body down the hill/*fall line*. You are now, as they say, "skiing in the backseat".

Pole plants in skiing are used for timing and balance. You plant the right pole and then turn right. You plant the left pole and then turn left. The pole plant occurs between turns. The exact timing is a personal preference. On moderate terrain the arms should remain still or quiet. A flick of the wrist is all that is needed to plant your pole. On steeper and more advanced terrain the pole plant may become more aggressive. Reaching down the hill for your pole plant on a very steep chute or a double pole plant to catch your balance, are good examples of this. When you are looking down hill, most of the time, you should be able to see your hands within your peripheral vision.

Throughout my 47 years of skiing I have seen that many skiers get stuck in the intermediate to advanced level of skiing. Five key points of awareness to focus on to help you break through getting stuck are:

1) FLEXION AND EXTENSION OR (WEIGHTING AND UNWEIGHTING)

It is important to flex your knees into the turn. It is just as important to extend out of it. When you pop out of a turn the skis are released from the snow. On groomed runs this can be very subtle, like peddling, but in crud or steep runs this pop out must be strong to release the skis. The skis can also be retracted (retraction turn) to release them from the snow.

2) FORWARD PRESSURE

This is mandatory for advanced to expert skiing. If your shins are not flexing into the ski boot and your hips are not being pushed forward, you are skiing in the back seat.

Regardless of the type of turn you are initiating, it is imperative to be in a forward centered position. Part of advancing to being an expert skier is knowing when and when not to carve a turn. On a steep and narrow chute you may be letting your skis slip sideways down the hill and or hopping your turns to an edge set to check speed. Also, when skiing *powder*, you do not have to carve your turns. These are but two examples of ski terrain when you have to use your skis to their full potential. It may take a little time to trust the *"A" Frame* body position, but that will come with experience.

3) ANGULATION

Angulation is key to carving a turn. To reiiterate, this means the downhill knee or both knees must be leaned into the turn and the upper body has to be facing down the hill. This knee and hip angulation is what creates a powerfully carved turn.

4) ROTATION

In most circumstances your feet/skis are rotating at the same rate in the direction you are turning. However, this is not always desirable. (please refer to pages 14 and 34 for the discussion of the *stem christie*/step turn, side slipping and *moguls*.

5) THE UPPER BODY – (HANDS, SHOULDERS, UPPER HIPS AND EYES)

The upper body must be facing down the *fall line*. Work hard on this one! It is critical for advanced to expert skiing. If all you do is get this one point, the rest will eventually come (Ah Ha :-). Have fun with it.

You can focus on these five points of awareness one at a time and as you master each one it will become easier to focus on all five. When you can do that, you're getting pretty darn good at skiing. At this point trust you know what you are doing and let it rip. You can always refer back to this pocket guide if you are having a hard time.

POWDER

Powder skiing, to some skiers, is the ultimate skiing experience. Other skiers find it incredibly difficult and challenging. The use of *"A" Frame Technique* with the following pointers should make powder skiing fun for all who wish to enjoy its beauty and grace.

There are many different types of *powder*. Sometimes the snow is light and fluffy and other times it is wet and heavy. It can also be anywhere in between those two extremes. After the *powder* has been skied through "cut up" as they say, it becomes a totally different experience, called *crud*.

The first thing to know is to go faster than you may think you want to. If you ski too slow, the skis will not float on and through the snow. Do not lean back on your skis. You do not have to be as far forward as when skiing on hard packed snow, but you do have to be in a forward position. If necessary, you can lift your toes in your boot, flexing the ankle and releasing pressure from the tip of the ski. When the skis are up out of, or towards the top of the snow, depending on snow conditions, is when you initiate the turn. Rotate your feet/ skis at the same rate in the direction you are turning. You then drop the skis into the turn crossing the *fall line*. If you can find a run that is not too steep, you can ski in a straight line, bouncing up and down with your skis through the snow to get the feel of this. In deep snow it is not necessary or desirable to sharply cross the *fall line*, the snow will help control your speed as the skis drop into it.

In *powder*, you may need to keep your skis very close together to get them to float through the snow. Your legs act like a shock absorber in a vehicle. They should be very stable from side to side and very flexible and strong up and down. Your hips should be driving forward and your upper body needs to point downhill. Let's say that again. Your upper body, (shoulders, hands, upper hips and eyes), need to point down the *fall line*. This can not be said too many times, it is critical to advanced skiing. (Photos on page 28 & 30 are of the Telemark turn)

MOGULS
Skiing the bumps

Skiing the bumps requires effort, agility, quickness and focus. There are different ways to navigate your way down a mogul field depending on your skiing ability level, physical fitness, age or degree of aggressiveness. Early in the learning curve, you may choose to traverse across the hill, around and over the bumps while absorbing them with your legs. As you progress, you can make longer radius turns around and over the bumps. The most aggressive way through moguls is down the *fall line* with short radius turns. This sometimes is referred to as the "zipper line." The moguls will probably not be in a perfect line, you need to be looking ahead and make adjustments as necessary.

First and foremost you need to be in the *"A" Frame* ski stance and using all the techniques discussed throughout this pocket guide. Just like in steep runs, any flaw in form will be magnified. Form is everything!

There are a few key points to focus on when skiing moguls.

1) KEEP YOUR SKIS ON THE SNOW AS MUCH AS POSSIBLE.

You must absorb the bumps with your legs and ankles as they impact the front or uphill side of the mogul. Then on the back or downhill side you must extend your legs and ankles to keep the skis and the ski tips in contact with the snow. (As in all sporting activities, do not overextend the knees. A straight knee is a vulnerable knee). The legs are the shock absorbers keeping the upper body as quiet/still as possible as they absorb the terrain. This is all done while turning the skis to control speed. Independent leg action is critical when skiing moguls.

2) DRIVE THE HIPS AND SKIS FORWARD.

The skis are driven forward from the hip and by extending the leg. This will keep you in a forward centered stance and create

a straighter carved turn. If you do not drive the skis forward, the skis will tend to wash/ slide out at the tail. Washing out at the tail may be a necessary maneuver at times to adjust to differing terrain and is a stepping stone in the learning curve. However, a carved turn is usually the most effective and efficient way to ski down a mountain with a solid like surface (not powder). If your hips are not pushed forward, your upper body will be bent over the skis instead of in a forward centered stance.

3) CHOOSING YOUR LINE.

As you stand at the top of a mogul field, look for and choose the line/route you plan to ski. This is also done when tree skiing. By picking a line/route, you have a general idea of what you are about to ski. However, on a long bump run with large moguls or in the trees, it is not possible to see all of the terrain changes. It is important to look ahead at the oncoming terrain.

4) POLE PLANTS AND TIMING.

As with all types of skiing, the pole plant is used for timing and balance. In general, the pole plant is a quick flick of the wrist, keeping the arms as quiet/still as you can. (See Seventh "A" Hands and Poles). You can only turn as fast as you can plant your poles. Because of this it is even more critical to have good hand position. Have fun in the bumps!

TELEMARK SKIING

The *telemark* turn is the original downhill ski turn. It has a beauty and grace to it both visually and in the feeling you get while skiing.

The big differences between the *alpine* and the *telemark* turn are:
1) A free heel *telemark* binding
2) The *telemark* boot
3) Leg and ski position
4) Weight distribution
5) Physical effort - harder on the muscles & gentler on the skeletal system

1) A free heel *telemark* binding is like a x-country binding, but much stronger. There are different types available, so it may be desirable to research *telemark* binding options.

2) The *telemark* boot flexes behind the toes.

3) Because of this free heel binding, your leg and ski positions are quite different than in *alpine* skiing. The inside/uphill knee of your turn is dropped down toward the outside/downhill heel, while simultaneously moving the inside foot backward and the outside foot forward (lead change). This is accomplished by a shuffling and extension/unweighting motion of your legs, feet and skis. Your uphill knee should be kept close to your downhill heel, as the stance should not be too spread apart. This makes for a powerful, tight and balanced body position. With *telemark* skiing, it is not always necessary to drop the knee all the way down to the snow or to the ski.

This can be practiced on dry land by jumping and shuffling the feet back and forth, such as in a lunge. While doing this jump/shuffle, rotate your lower body left and then right, to mimic turning and separating the lower and upper body. You can then practice this with your skis on a shallow slope at low speed without the turning. Next, add a little angulation, then rotation as you perform the lead change to initiate a turn. There are three types of lead change; 1)shuffling as in a "scissoring" motion, 2)forward momentum (moving the rear foot forward), and 3)moving the front foot back. The scissor and the forward momentum lead changes are the higher performing maneuvers, while the backwards change is good to check speed or for added quickness when needed.

4) Your weight should be evenly distributed on both feet and skis. This is the optimal and most stable distribution of weight. In some circumstances it may be necessary to put more weight (60/40%) on your inside/uphill ski. This may seem counterintuitive, but because of the separation of upper and lower body, this is where your weight wants to fall if you are facing your shoulders, hands, upper hips and eyes downhill. You can try this in your dry land practice to get a feel for it and see how it works. This weight distribution will become imperative in advanced and steep terrain. (This is contrary to some teaching methods that say to put more weight on your outside ski.) Give both a try and see what works for you in advanced terrain.

When you get on the snow, you will find that the *telemark* equipment will make *alpine* turns. Many people like to fall back to this form when they feel they need to.

To get started with the *telemark* turn, a good stepping stone is to start in a *wedge* position on a shallow to moderate slope. Go ahead and make a few *wedge* turns to get the feel of your equipment. Now, while skiing

in a *wedge* turn, after you have pointed your skis down the hill, shuffle your inside ski back a little by dropping your inside knee.

Keep your weight balanced on both skis and face your upper body down the hill/ *fall line* while you rotate your lower body and skis in the direction you are turning. If your knees are not angulated into the turn, your turn will have a side slipping motion to it. To carve the turn, you must angulate both knees into the turn. This is done with knee and hip angulation. Remember your upper body position and drive your inside shoulder down the hill. This will put your shoulders perpendicular to the *fall line*.

Just like *alpine* skiing, you need to down weight/flex into the turn and unweight/extend out of the turn. It is in the extension/unweighting, that you shuffle and start rotating the skis to their new position for the next turn. Retracting the skis also works (retraction turn). The pole plant motion is the same as is in alpine, as is the pressuring of the skis throughout the carve, with the exception of the 50/50% ski weight distribution.

Holding a carved turn is where that infamous *telemark* leg burn occurs. Your turns can be hoppy short swing or long graceful arched carves, or anything in between. The extension/unweighting can be very strong for crud and steep skiing or very subtle on a groomed run. Of course, powder is the best. Powder skiing techniques are very similar on telemark skis. See *Powder* on page 30.

Have fun and happy trails!

THANK YOU . . .

Thank you to my family members who supported and guided me throughout this project: my partner Sascha Meier, my three children – Nick Hernon, Meadow Sylvan, and Lyric Sylvan.

I also thank my "old school" twin brother Joe Hernon, and a special thanks to my mother Ellyn Hernon Dekker, for her outstanding editing skills and for driving her children to the local ski area every weekend of the winter.

Thank you, Harvey Meier, for your wonderful advice, and thank you, Deborah Perdue, for your guidance and design skills.

TO PURCHASE

To integrate Bill Hernon's Modern "A" Frame Ski Technique into a professional school methodology, please email bill@skiaframe.com

To order a soft copy or ebook of this pocket guide, please log into www.skiaframe.com/pocketguide

www.ingramcontent.com/pod-product-compliance
Lightning Source LLC
Chambersburg PA
CBHW050018040726
47599CB00014B/1452